SONGS FOR SIGHT-SINGIN VOLUME 2

High School/Junior High School — SAB

Compiled by
Mary Henry and Marilyn Jones

Consulting Editor
Dr. Ruth Whitlock

Director of Music Education Studies
Texas Christian University

SOUTHERN MUSIC COMPANY
Publishing Division

Preface

The anthologies SONGS FOR SIGHT-SINGING
and SONGS FOR SIGHT-SINGING Volume 2
provide a collection of literature for use in the
choral classroom. Each selection was composed
according to criteria designed by Texas secondary
choral directors and commissioned by the
University of Texas Interscholastic League for
use in its annual sight singing contest. These
graded materials were created specifically for
young musicians by recognized composers and
comprise a valuable resource as they contain
many of the problems encountered in sight
singing. This collection can be used effectively as
a supplement to the daily instructional sight
singing program after an approved system of
pitch reference (movable "do", fixed "do" or
numbers) and a rhythm system are established
within the choral curriculum.

Table of Contents

ANGEL SONG, Council 68
BEHOLD A STAR, Crocker 64
CALL, THE, Crocker 5
CHILDREN'S PRAYER, DeWitt 12
EVENING, Williams-Wimberly 73
HOUSE ON THE HILL, THE, Land 24
IRISH BLESSING, AN, DeWitt 8
LORD IS MY STRENGTH, THE, Riley 35
MEET ME, DeWitt 28
MOTHER'S LOVE, Siltman 16
MY HEART'S IN THE HIGHLANDS, Land 44
MY LOVE ASLEEP DOTH LIE, Shearer 61
MY LOVE IS LIKE A RED, RED ROSE,
      Williams-Wimberly 58
NIGHTFALL, Williams-Wimberly 40
OH, LITTLE ONE, Riley 32
PRAISE THE NAME OF THE LORD, Riley 48
REJOICE, OH EARTH! Riley 20
SINCE FIRST I SAW YOUR FACE, Leininger 78
TO THEE, OH LORD, Crocker 54

B520

The Call

GEORGE HERBERT
(1593-1632)

EMILY CROCKER

B520

ends all strife, such _____ a life as kill - eth death.
mends in length, such _____ a strength as makes his guest.

ends all strife, _____ such a life as kill - eth death.
mends in length, _____ such a strength as makes his guest.

ends all strife, such _____ a life as kill - eth death.
mends in length, such _____ a strength as makes his guest.

Come my joy, my love, my heart: such _____ a

Come my joy, my love, my heart: such a

Come my joy, my love, my heart: such _____ a

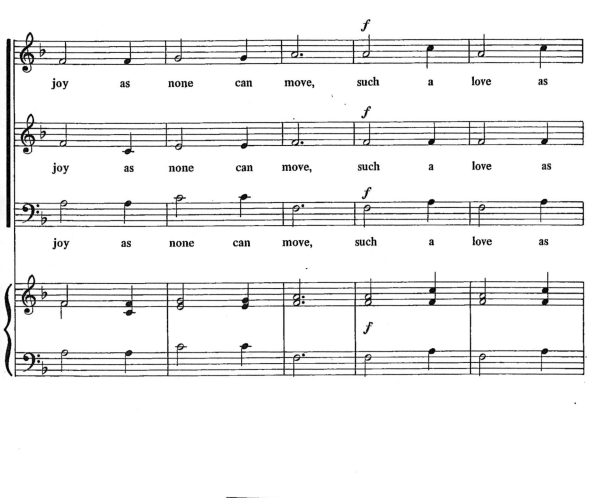

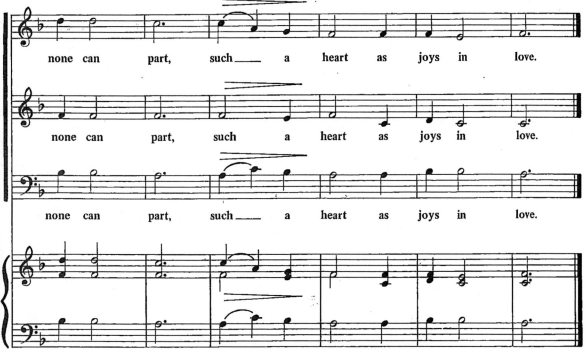

B520

An Irish Blessing

TRADITIONAL
revised by PATTI DEWITT

PATTI DEWITT

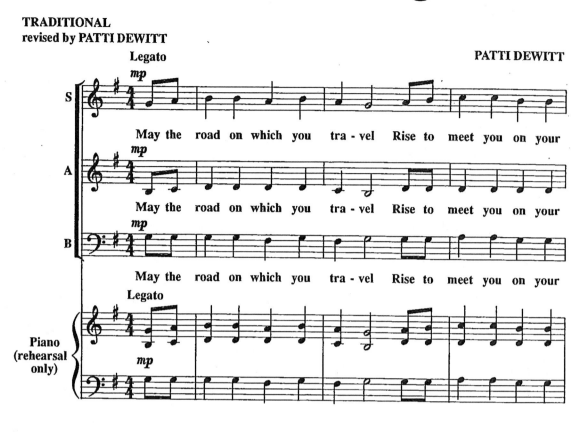

Piano
(rehearsal
only)

May the road on which you tra-vel Rise to meet you on your

May the road on which you tra-vel Rise to meet you on your

May the road on which you tra-vel Rise to meet you on your

way. May the gen-tle wind be-hind you Help you

way. May the gen-tle wind be-hind you Help you

way. May the gen-tle wind be-hind you Help you

B520

make it thru' the day. May the warm and balm - y

make it thru' the __ day. May the warm and balm - y

make it thru' the day. May the warm and balm - y

sun - shine Light your face with gol - den glow. May the soft, re - fresh - ing

sun - shine Light your face with gol - den glow. May the soft, re - fresh - ing

sun - shine Light your face with gol - den glow. May the soft, re - fresh - ing

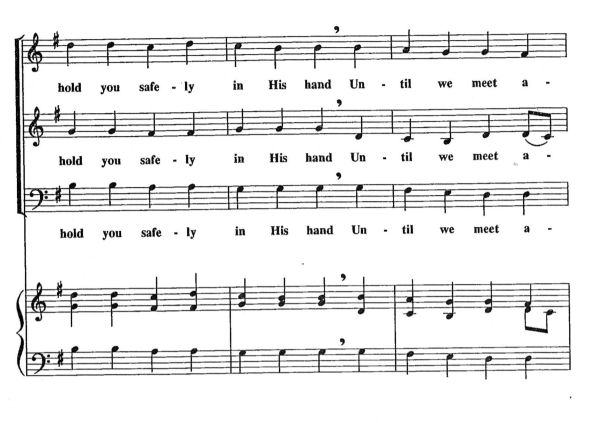

Children's Prayer

**Adapted from
"HANSEL & GRETEL"**

PATTI DEWITT

14

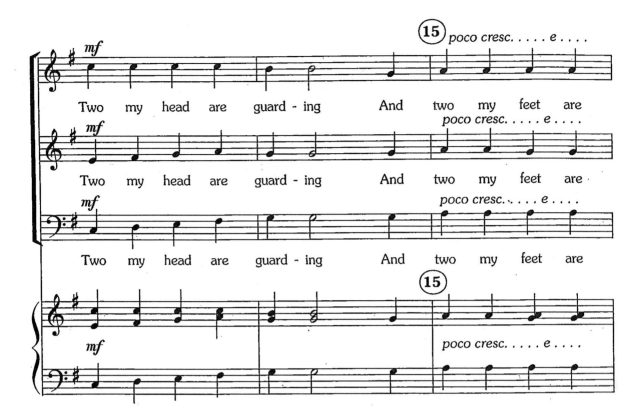

poco cresc. . . . . e . . . .

Two my head are guard-ing And two my feet are

Two my head are guard-ing And two my feet are

Two my head are guard-ing And two my feet are

guid - ing. Two who 'round me hov - er,

guid - ing. Two who 'round me hov - er, ___

guid - ing. Two who 'round me hov - er,

B520

MOTHER'S LOVE

UNKNOWN　　　　　　　　　　　　　　　　　　**BOBBY SILTMAN**

Her love is like an is - land in life's o - cean wide. A

peace - ful qui - et shel - ter from wind, rain, and tide. Bound

Rejoice, Oh Earth!

Words and Music by
SHARI RILEY

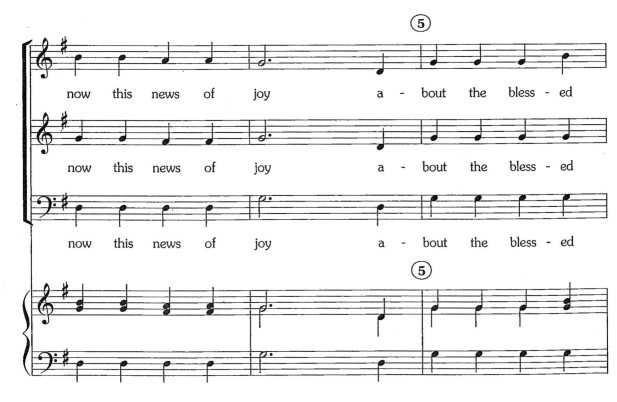

The House on the Hill

EDWIN ARLINGTON ROBINSON
Adapted by Lois Land

LOIS LAND

26

B520

MEET ME

Words and Music by
PATTI DEWITT

B520

30

B520

pledge our love for - ev - er - more, and we shall be as

pledge our love for - ev - er - more, and we shall be as

pledge our love for - ev - er - more, and we shall be as

(25) cresc. _ f

one. And we shall be as one.

cresc. _ f

one. And we shall be as one.

cresc. _ f

one. And we shall be as one.

(25)

cresc. _ f

Oh Little One

Words and Music by
SHARI RILEY

THE LORD IS MY STRENGTH AND STAY

Words & Music by
SHARI RILEY

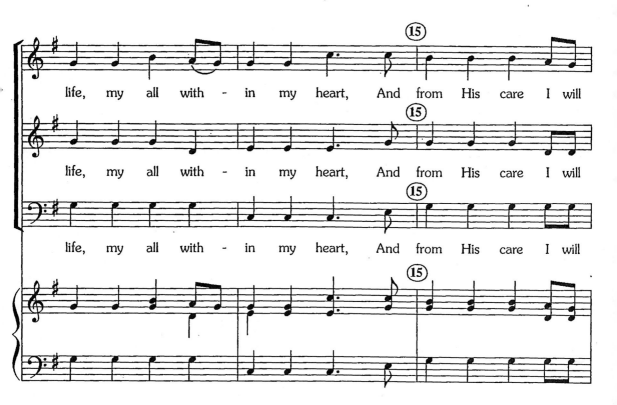

life, my all with - in my heart, And from His care I will

life, my all with - in my heart, And from His care I will

life, my all with - in my heart, And from His care I will

nev - er de - part. Oh Al - might - y Lord,

nev - er de - part. Oh Al - might - y Lord,

nev - er de - part. Oh Al - might - y Lord,

Most Ho - ly One; Ma - jes - ty a - dored,

Most Ho - ly One; Ma - jes - ty a - dored,

Most Ho - ly One;_____ Ma - jes - ty a - dored,

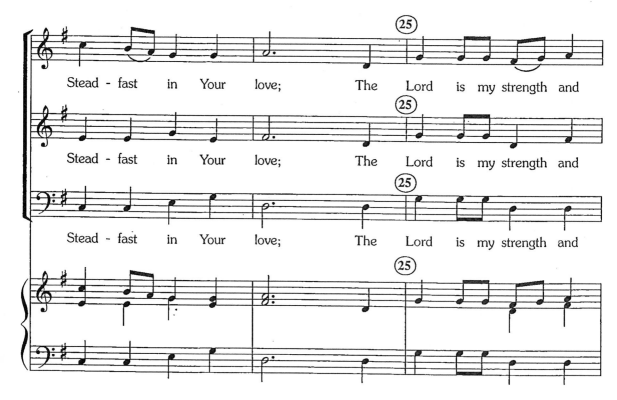

Stead - fast in Your love; The Lord is my strength and

Stead - fast in Your love; The Lord is my strength and

Stead - fast in Your love; The Lord is my strength and

Nightfall

HENRY WADSWORTH LONGFELLOW

LOU WILLIAMS-WIMBERLY

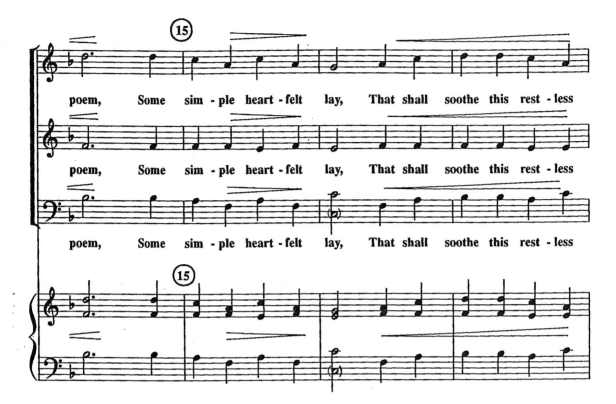

poem,   Some   sim - ple heart - felt   lay,   That shall   soothe this   rest - less

poem,   Some   sim - ple heart - felt   lay,   That shall   soothe this   rest - less

poem,   Some   sim - ple heart - felt   lay,   That shall   soothe this   rest - less

feel - ing And   ban - ish the thoughts   of   day.   And   then   the

feel - ing And   ban - ish the thoughts   of   day.   And   then   the

feel - ing And   ban - ish the thoughts   of   day.   And   then   the

night shall be filled with mu - sic That will qui - et my ev - 'ry care, And

night shall be filled with mu - sic That will qui - et my ev - 'ry care, And

night shall be filled with mu - sic That will qui - et my ev - 'ry care, And

come like the ben - e - dic - tion That fol - lows af - ter pray'r.

come like the ben - e - dic - tion That fol - lows af - ter pray'r.

come like the ben - e - dic - tion That fol - lows af - ter pray'r.

My Heart's in the Highlands

ROBERT BURNS

LOIS LAND

48

Praise the Name of the Lord!

Words and Music by
SHARI RILEY

To Thee, O Lord, Our Hearts We Raise

SAB

WM. DIX (1837-1898)

EMILY CROCKER

Stately (♩ = 84)

strains of all its ho - ly throng with ours to - day are blend - ing, Thrice

strains of all its ho - ly throng with ours to - day are blend - ing, Thrice

strains of all its ho - ly throng with ours to - day are blend - ing, Thrice

bless - ed is that har - vest song which nev - er hath an end - ing.

bless - ed is that har - vest song which nev - er hath an end - ing.

bless - ed is that har - vest song which nev - er hath an end - ing.

My Love is Like a Red, Red Rose

ROBERT BURNS

LOU WILLIAMS - WIMBERLY

Lyrical ♩ = 72

O my love is like a red, red rose That is new-ly sprung in June; O my
As___ fair you are, my bon-nie lass, So___ deep in love am I; And___

love is like the mel-o-dy That is sweet-ly played in tune.
I will love you still my dear, Till ___ all the seas go dry.

MY LOVE ASLEEP DOTH LIE

THE SPECTATOR (c. 1775)

C.M. SHEARER

62

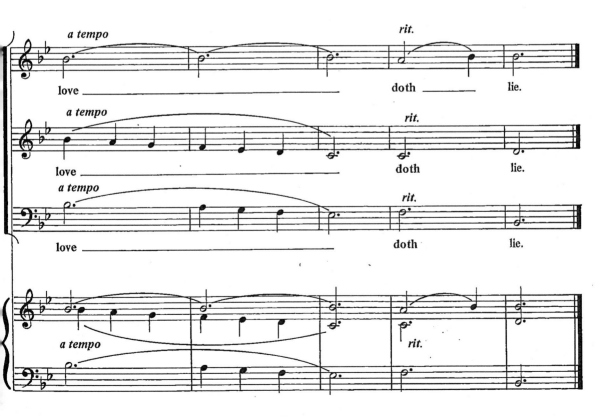

Behold A Star

SAB

WM. DIX (1837-1898)

EMILY CROCKER

B520

Angel Song

Words and Music by
TOM COUNCIL

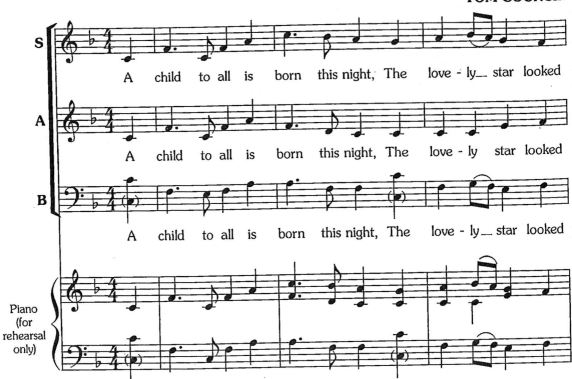

calm — and — bright, God came to — all this night.

calm and — bright, God came to all this night.

calm and — bright, God came to — all this night. Glad

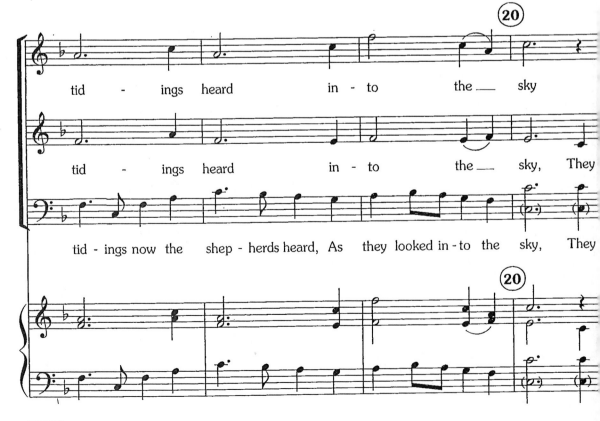

tid - ings heard in - to the — sky

tid - ings heard in - to the — sky, They

tid - ings now the shep - herds heard, As they looked in - to the sky, They

72

B520

Evening
(In Words of One Syllable)

THOMAS MILLER

LOU WILLIAMS - WIMBERLY

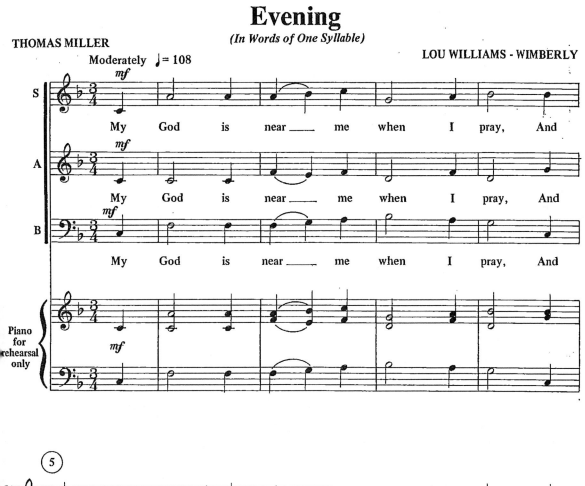

My God is near____ me when I pray, And

when I close____ my eyes in sleep, I know that

76

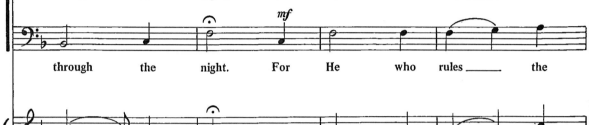

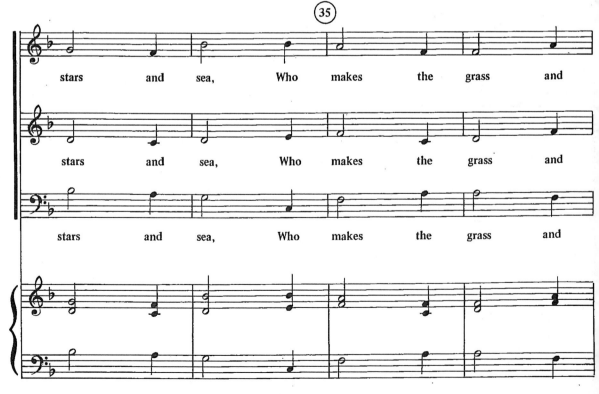

B520

trees   to   grow,   Will   look   on   a   poor   child   like

trees   to   grow,   Will   look   on   a   poor   child   like

trees   to   grow,   Will   look   on   a   poor   child   like

rit.

me,   When   on   my   knees   I   to   Him   bow.

rit.

me,   When   on   my   knees   I   to   Him   bow.

rit.

me,   When   on   my   knees   I   to   Him   bow.

rit.

Since First I Saw Your Face

THOMAS FORD

JIM LEININGER

heart had nev - er known ye. What, I that loved and
my poor eyes the bold - er, Where beau - ty moves and

heart had nev - er known ye. What, I that loved and
my poor eyes the bold - er, Where beau - ty moves and

heart had nev - er known ye. What, I that loved and
my poor eyes the bold - er, Where beau - ty moves and

mf

you that liked, shall we be - gin to wran - gle? No, no, no, my
wit de - lights, and signs of kind - ness bind me, There, O there, where

mf

you that liked, shall we be - gin to wran - gle? No, no, no, my
wit de - lights, and signs of kind - ness bind me, There, O there, where

mf

you that liked, shall we be - gin to wran - gle? No, no, no, my
wit de - lights, and signs of kind - ness bind me, There, O there, where

mf

B520

heart is fast, and can - not dis - en - tan - gle.
e'er I go, I leave my heart be - hind me,

heart is fast, and can - not dis - en - tan - gle.
e'er I go, I leave my heart be - hind me.

heart is fast, and can - not dis - en - tan - gle.
e'er I go, I leave my heart be - hind me.

No, no, no, my heart is fast, and can - not dis - en - tan - gle.
There, O there, where - e'er I go, I leave my heart be - hind me.

No, no, no, my heart is fast, and can - not dis - en - tan - gle.
There, O there, where - e'er I go, I leave my heart be - hind me.

No, no, no, my heart is fast, and can - not dis - en - tan - gle.
There, O there, where - e'er I go, I leave my heart be - hind me.